BACK POCKET

BACK POCKET

Tools for Teens Struggling with Their Mental Health

SHANEY ANDLER

gatekeeper press

Columbus, Ohio

BACK POCKET

Tools for Teens Struggling with Their Mental Health

Published by Gatekeeper Press

2167 Stringtown Rd., Suite 109

Columbus, OH 43123-2989

www.GatekeeperPress.com

The cover design, interior formatting, typesetting, and editorial work for this book are entirely the product of the author. Gatekeeper Press did not participate in and is not responsible for any aspect of these elements.

Library of Congress Control Number: 2022937591

ISBN (paperback): 9781662928376

eISBN: 9781662932014

Praise for *Back Pocket*

"The first thing that goes when we are under stress is our ability to think. Going back to the basics and having simple, concrete strategies to try and get us out of our reptilian brain is so important to help get unstuck."

—Kathy, certified child therapist

"This book was something I definitely would have used and needed. I probably still will at some point."

—Alex, 22

"What a gift to our youth!"

—high school counselor

"Back Pocket is teaching the same things we are teaching here (DBT, CBT), but just saying it differently."

—hospital inpatient unit certified therapist

"It was so relatable."

—mother of 2 teen boys

"Shaney provides personal experience and professional expertise in ways that are incredibly helpful and useful for parents and practitioners who want to support students who are struggling with their mental health challenges. Her no-nonsense and relatable style make Back Pocket a necessary resource for kids, families and educators."

—Dana Monogue, Superintendent of Middleton Cross Plains Area School District

"The length is appreciated."

—8th grade student

"It's something I will keep going back to."

—11th grade student

"My daughter NEEDS these basic skills and that is the key to why this book is so good."

—father of 15 year old girl

FOREWARD

———

Throughout the 20+ years I have worked as a high school counselor, what I have learned is that when a student feels empowered they begin to understand that they have more control over their mental well-being than they first realized. In fact, I have witnessed many of the strategies in *Back Pocket* work for students, and I am grateful to Shaney for putting this all together in such an accessible way.

Shaney is someone who practices what she preaches. She has spent years being the scientist and the experiment as she researches and tests out practical straightforward ways for people of all ages to reduce their stress and take control of their well-being.

Shaney has a gift for connecting with others and as you read *Back Pocket*, it will truly feel like Shaney is walking alongside you, helping you navigate some of the stressors you are facing. Shaney has invited us into her life and there is comfort in the way that she models vulnerability. I think of how much we could learn from each other and connect more deeply with others if we all were willing to tell our stories and make time for others as Shaney does.

Back Pocket provides many useful, sound, and practical ideas that are research-based. They are the type of strategies a student can grab a hold of at any moment. I believe students will find relief in Shaney's unique and shame-free approach to working through mental health challenges.

In just a few minutes you will learn how to take back control and ease the stressors in your lives. This is truly a journey worth taking. I want to remind our youth that they have exactly what they need. They are whole and have more control then they may realize over their well-being and health.

Gust Athanas, MS.Ed., NCC, NCSC
Board Certified School Counselor

This book is not intended to be a diagnostic tool, a cure, or a replacement for professional care.

While I wholeheartedly agree with professional help, I also agree that there are some simple things that can promote change too.

I am not a therapist, doctor, or psychologist, just a mom and teacher who has lived with someone who struggles and has worked with lots of struggling kids. Physical trainers at gyms are not cardiologists, yet they help you take care of your heart, right? Think of this book as your physical trainer then. I have seen the things in this book work firsthand and have organized and compiled them in the hopes that they help you.

TABLE OF CONTENTS

————

INTRODUCTION

————

L et's see if you are in the right place.

Do you feel like your mental health is getting in the way of your normal life?

Are you experiencing unpleasant feelings and thoughts that are new?

Do you feel like you don't know what to do about it?

Do you feel like you wish you had some strategies and tools to help yourself?

If you said "yes" to any of these, this book is for you.

I See you. I hear you.
You matter.

The reason I wrote this book is because my son, Alex, has struggled with some mental health issues in the past. Kindergarten was bad, second grade was worse, and seventh grade was the worst. As a parent, I didn't know how to help him. We struggled to find materials out there that gave him strategies to try on the spot. I found a lot of books that described what was going on and other books that gave motivational encouragement.

I stumbled upon some workbooks, but Alex wanted no part of those. I was paralyzed in how to help him feel better, and I wished I could just give him some tools for his "back pocket" to reference and access when he needed them. I eventually found a therapist, and Alex went weekly for a year. This therapist was perfect for my son and gave him the tools he needed. However, he had to work at it. It was not a quick fix, and it was not handed to him. He learned and practiced and practiced some more.

We live in a world today where we have quick fixes. We want Chipotle, so we order Uber Eats. We want an answer to something, and we look it up on Google. If we want to watch a show everyone is talking about, we stream it right then and there. Heck, if we need grey salt from France, we order it on Amazon, and it shows up the next day.

Health does not work that way. I have always compared mental health to physical health because you need to take care of it. We proactively exercise to prevent disease and going to the hospital. I think we should be the exact same way with mental health. If you don't take care of it and nurture it, it can spiral out of control and affect you negatively. But what comes with that is work. I'm sorry, but there is no quick fix to making yourself better. No one is going to do it for you.

When Alex was at his worst with his anxiety, we compared it to being on a hamster wheel. It was really hard for him to work and help himself when that wheel was spinning so fast. The wheel needed to slow down in order for his mind to be ready to do some work. You may be on that hamster wheel right now, so jump in slowly. By that, I mean do not read this book and think, "I need to learn all of those tools right now." That's totally not going to work. In fact, my recommendation is to skim through them all and focus on one. Practice, perfect, and execute!

That is how you do other things in life, right? Can you imagine if you played four sports? You wouldn't really be able to focus on one; you'd just sort of skim the surface of all of them.

It's the same with playing four instruments, studying for four huge tests, or playing four video games.

After that experience with my son, I immersed myself in the area of teen mental health. I educated myself, and I talked to hundreds of kids and even more parents. I realized that we were facing a really big issue, and I wanted to make a change. So many of the solutions seemed to be reactive: therapy, hospital visits, and medication. While these solutions are absolutely critical to many teens' journeys, my goal is to be PROACTIVE and give you tools before you are in a spot where you feel completely hopeless.

Which brings me to *Back Pocket*. This book is intended to give you tools for your "back pocket." These are things that can be done right here, right now; and will be with you wherever you go. I chose the four tools specifically because I wanted them to be easy. I wanted them to be inclusive so anyone, anywhere can do them, and most importantly, I wanted them to be effective. These were the four that I have seen work with Alex and other struggling kids. I tried to keep the book pretty short. Some of you may love to read (Kudos to you; it will pay off for you in so many ways!), but some of you may dread it like my two boys. This book is also intended to be a reference guide. Highlight it, mark your favorite chapters, and come back to it whenever you need to. And always remember, what works for someone else may not work for you!

You are on a journey right now. You are figuring out that life can be hard, but you are making an effort to help yourself just by opening this book. That, my friend, is the very first step.

Tool #1

ACCESSING YOUR "HAPPY HORMONES"

What the heck are "happy hormones"? You don't need to know exactly what they are, only that they are how we tap into feelings. There are very detailed and in-depth reasons for the release of hormones in the body, but honestly, they are way over my head. I'm in no position to teach you. What I do know is that hormones don't discriminate, so every single person has them and can access them in some way. I think of a water bottle when I think of hormones, picturing the water squeezing out the top. That is like what is happening inside your brain. The great thing is that we have the power to release these hormones on our own, and I am going to teach you how.

A few years ago, I started a club at our local high school called Bridge Club. It's a club where we teach and show kids how to access their happy hormones. We meet weekly and actively access these hormones by making jewelry, taking walks, talking and laughing, eating, listening to music, doing volunteer projects, and more. My goal of Bridge Club is that kids find something that works for them. They find that one thing that made them feel a certain way: good, relaxed, happy, distracted, etc.

One of the main reasons for writing this book is to bring Bridge Club to you. I have done so much research on this topic and have seen amazing things happen among kids when they engage in this process.

There are four hormones that fall into the happy hormones category: dopamine, oxytocin, serotonin, and endorphins (DOSE). These hormones are released in different ways by doing everyday things. The thing I love about the happy hormones tool is that it can be done anywhere, alone or with people, and can be done immediately. You don't need to attend a class, have an appointment, or wait for a certain day or time to do these things. Here are the four hormone descriptions and how to access them. It's easy-peasy.

Oxytocin

Oxytocin is known as the "cuddle" or love hormone. It plays a role in bonding and relationships.

Here are some ways to access oxytocin:

- *physical touch*
- *socializing*
- *massage*
- *acupuncture*
- *listening to music*
- *exercise*
- *playing with a dog*
- *playing with a baby*
- *holding a hand*
- *giving a hug*
- *giving a compliment*
- *dancing*
- *volunteering or helping others*

Endorphins

Endorphins are known as the calm hormones. They help you to relieve stress and pain and give you a feeling of euphoria and pleasure.

Here are some ways to access endorphins:

- *laughing*
- *crying*
- *eating spicy foods*
- *exercise*
- *stretching*
- *massage*
- *meditation*
- *essential oils*
- *doing something creative*
- *eating dark chocolate*

Dopamine

Dopamine is known as the reward hormone and is responsible for feelings of pleasure and satisfaction. It also affects motivation and concentration.

Here are some ways to access dopamine:

- *completing a task*
- *eating food*
- *self-care activities*
- *celebrating little wins*
- *gratitude*
- *exercise*
- *reaching a goal*

Serotonin

Serotonin is known as the willpower hormone and is responsible for mood, memory, sleep, appetite, and social behavior. It gives you a sense of well-being and is the hormone most affected by diet. A good diet equals good serotonin.

Here are some ways to access serotonin:

- *being in sunlight*
- *exercise*
- *meditation*
- *sleep*
- *laughter*
- *spending time in nature*
- *cold showers*
- *massage*

I know that ....
helps me when I feel ....

This is a sentence that is so, so, so important. It brings an awareness that is actually quite powerful. You very well may not know how to fill in those blanks yet, but be patient. It takes time. My sentence would look like this:

*I know that **listening to music really loud in my car**
helps me when I feel **stressed.***

My sentence is mine and does not work for everyone, which is why this is so important. Hopefully, this happy hormone section will make you aware that there are scientifically proven ways to release your happy hormones to make you feel happier and more relaxed, and it is your job to find out what works for you.

Tool # 2

FOUR STRATEGIES
TO TRY

———

Breathing

I feel like breathing is one of those things we say a lot, like "Take a deep breath," but don't really focus and concentrate on. Once you learn to do this—wow, good for you. It's an instant way to feel a little better.

When my son was struggling, he always said he felt like he couldn't breathe. He actually was right; he couldn't. He was breathing but not actually taking breaths. Here is why:

When you are nervous, anxious, sad, etc., your body tenses up. When everything is tight, your lungs don't have room to expand.

Tighten up your core like you are bracing for someone to punch you in the stomach. Now, with your body tight, try to take a deep breath. You can't, right?

That is exactly what is going on with your body when you are anxious, and it's one of the main symptoms of panic attacks. So, the very first thing I tell kids when they are anxious is, "Let's start with some breathing." Here are a few easy breathing exercises:

1. The "7-4-8" Exercise

Take a slow deep breath through your nose for seven seconds. When you get your lungs completely expanded, hold your breath for four seconds. Exhale your breath out of your mouth for a count of eight seconds, making sure every last piece of air is out. Try to do this three times.

2. The Melting Ice Cream Exercise

Take a deep breath in. As you exhale, focus on a part of your body, (I like to focus on my face first.) totally relaxing and turning into melting ice cream. Go through a few more breaths, focusing on other parts of your body. Do this until you feel a little more relaxed. You can feel your-self just loosening up.

3. The Balloon Exercise

Imagine a huge balloon inside your body. Think of it going from your chest down to your belly button.

When you inhale, the balloon in your chest and abdomen area completely inflates, and when you exhale, it deflates.

....

You do not need to do all of these exercises. I gave you three different examples because what might work for you may not work for someone else. The key to these, though, is to really focus on them. It's called mind-body connection. Whatever you need to do to tune out any distractions, do it. Lock yourself in a room, go into your car, go under your bed covers, or whatever. I also am a big fan of the apps today that give you specific breathing exercises or meditations and even tell you relaxing stories. I listen to them every night before bed. These breathing exercise suggestions are intended to relax you so you can go on to one of the next strategies.

Distraction

Distraction sounds easy, doesn't it? Well, when your mind is going, it can be very difficult. Distraction is not meant to ignore an issue; it is just meant to redirect your mind for the time being.

Distraction can be something as easy as changing your environment. If you are in your room and your mind is going, go to the family room or basement. Just the act of walking somewhere else or looking at a new wall helps.

Distraction can also be something as easy as taking a shower or changing your clothes. Here are some games you can try which are sort of fun:

- *Starting at a hundred, subtract by sevens down to zero.*
- *Starting at Z, say the alphabet backwards.*
- *Starting with your left little toe, move each one individually.*
- *Think of a person's name for every letter of the alphabet.*
- *Think of ten to twenty songs your favorite artist sings.*

Again, you do not need to sit and do all of these. One might work for you, or they may not work at all. That is OK. That is why this book gives you lots and lots of options to help yourself.

Play the "Rationalize Game"

This is basically just using your common sense. You are all smart kids. After all, you are reading this book! So, you need to ask yourself some hard, honest questions and answer with honest answers. Here are two questions to ask, and I'm going to walk you through some example questions and answers:

1. What is the worst that can happen?

"What is the worst that can happen if I don't make the sports team or if I don't play well?"

- *"People will think I suck." Nope, that's not true.*

- *"My parents will be mad." Maybe, but they'll get over it.*

- *"I'll never get to play on this team, or I will get cut." Life will go on.*

"What is the worst that can happen if my friend is mad at me?"

- *"They will talk about me to my other friends." Your friends are old enough to make their own decisions.*

- *"I won't get to hang out with them anymore, and they're fun." Lots of people are fun.*

"I got caught cheating at school and I am in trouble. What's the worst that can happen?" Well, you did do something wrong, so take the punishment and move on. You will forget about it quickly.

See how that works? When you go down the path of "The worst that can happen is . . . ," you prepare yourself for the worst, which usually doesn't sound so bad when you think it through. When you are prepared for the worst, well then, things can only go up from there! Prepare for the worst, and hope for the best!

2.   What are the chances that will happen?

- *"I have a fear of dying." Think of all of the kids you know, and think of how many you know that have died.*

- *"My friends will never talk to me again." Really, really think about that. Never? Trust me, they will.*

- *"My bad decision will affect my whole life." Think of how many bad decisions are made every day.*

Basically, this strategy is just you talking through issues in your head. If you really think hard about things, they seem to fix themselves in a way. And if they don't fix themselves, at least you have processed it internally and, again, almost prepared yourself. Do you know that many times worrying is just you preparing yourself for the worst possible situation? That way if your "worry" were to happen, you are not caught off guard.

Help Someone Else

This is actually my favorite strategy as I am a firm believer in volunteering and helping others. I would go so far as to say it's almost impossible not to feel better after helping someone else. Research has shown that by volunteering you are actually lowering your risk for depression and anxiety. I always call volunteering "helping yourself by helping others." I also think random acts of kindness fall into this category. They make you feel so good!

You are probably saying, "I want to volunteer, but I don't know where to go or who to call." That is very common, so I am going to give you a few examples that you can try:

- *Message a friend who you know is having a hard time right now. Just an "I'm thinking of you today." goes a really long way. Did that feel good? Message another.*

- *Local humane societies are always looking for people to make cat beds. These are the fleece blankets that you tie together on the ends. If you go to a fabric store like*

JOANN and buy a yard of fleece, you can make one! The directions are right on the Humane Society's website, and when you are finished, you can drop them off.

- *Walk through your neighborhood and pick up some trash. You'd be amazed at how much is on the ground once you start looking!*

- *Go talk to the special needs teacher at your school. They are always looking for peers to assist with their students, and it is very hands-on and extremely rewarding!*

- *Do you have an elderly neighbor? If you knock on their door and ask them if they need any help, I can almost guarantee they will need help. Sometimes they just ask for a weekly phone call because they are so lonely.*

- *Write five notes, and put them in random people's lockers or under their windshield wipers on their car. I'm pretty sure you will make their day even though it came from a stranger.*

- *Even simple things like smiling at someone, giving a compliment, or helping someone who dropped something make a difference and make you feel better. Sometimes, I feel like volunteering can seem overwhelming, but I do believe you get what you give. Little things make us all feel better about ourselves!*

So there you go, four strategies to try. As I said before, they may not work immediately, but remember, we are not looking for that quick fix. You may have to try some a few times to find the benefits. It's a marathon, not a sprint!

Tool #3

FINDING AND RECOGNIZING GRATITUDE

———

Gratitude is definitely one of those trendy words being thrown around these days. The definition of gratitude is "the quality of being thankful, readiness to show appreciation for and to return kindness." It's actually a quite powerful tool in helping you feel better, but it is not meant to make you feel guilty.

There is an old saying by Leo Tolstoy that goes, "I cried because I had no shoes until I met a man who had no feet." While this saying is very true, that there is always someone worse off than you, it sometimes makes kids feel bad. We are always told to be grateful for what we have, but does that necessarily mean that just because we have enough food, a roof over our head, and a family that we don't struggle? Absolutely not! Everyone struggles, regardless of what you have. So, let's look at gratitude in two different ways: gratitude for the little things in life and finding positivity.

Gratitude for Little Things

When people are asked what they are grateful for, most immediately say, "My family, my friends, and my pet," but I like to call those things "givens." Givens are things that you will always be grateful for, so they are just assumed. When I ask kids to tell me three things they are grateful for, I have them think, really think, of what they are grateful for that day. I'm going to play this game right now for myself.

"Shaney, what are you grateful for today?" After stopping to really think, here are my answers:

- *Even though it was yesterday, I had the best butterscotch ice cream cone I ever had. I am grateful that this butterscotch ice cream exists because now I can enjoy it lots more.*

- *I am going to dinner tonight with a friend I haven't seen in a really long time.*

- *My dog got a good report yesterday from the vet, even though they had been worried about something on her neck.*

So you see, even though I talked about my friends and my pet, it was something specific that applied that day. These little things can be:

- *The weather allows for my window to be open in my room.*
- *I'm having a good hair day.*
- *I got a good grade on an assignment.*
- *Someone gave me a compliment.*
- *My stomach doesn't hurt today.*

Many people use journaling to help with this by actually writing three things down. You can get a fancy gratitude journal or just use a plain notebook. I think it is fun to look back on these things. However, many of you do not love to write, and you do not need to! Just thinking these things in your head is effective too. It's a mindset.

1. ....
2. ....
3. ....

Finding Positivity

This is similar to gratitude, in a way. Finding positivity requires you again to stop and think, really think. Many times, worrying, anxiety, and depression make people very negative. They see the bad in everything. I get it; their life sort of stinks right now. One thing to think about, though, is what kind of people do you like to be around: people who see the good or people that bring you down? It's not your job to make others happy, but that line of thinking may push you into being more positive. It's something to think about.

In the same way you perform the gratitude exercise, you will perform the positive exercise.

Many times, people ask you to think or say three positive things about yourself, but you may not be feeling that right now.

When I don't feel up to that, it can also work like this: taking something negative and putting a positive spin on it. Here is how this works:

"Shaney, think of three positive things." I stop and think of these answers:

- *My fingers hurt from typing, but I know it's good because I am writing this book.*
- *It's raining today, but that means spring flowers will come up soon.*
- *I need to go to the grocery store, but then I will have all the ingredients to make soup tonight.*

I took three negative things and looked for the positives in them. If you cannot find good in the negative you thought of, move on to something else.

When kids I work with are being overly negative, I will have them stop talking, think of ways to change the negative into positive, and then tell me about it. Their demeanor changes almost immediately. There have been scientific studies to show that having a positive attitude affects you not only mentally but physically. You get sick less if you are a positive person!

Tool #4

PUT DOWN THE PHONE

B efore I start, I want to say I am addicted to my phone too. I am not going to preach (well, maybe a little) about how phones are evil and no one should ever use them again. I'm sure you've heard it many times already from parents, family, guardians, teachers, and coaches. I say the same things to my kids. However, I do believe it's true. Unfortunately, I think they are pretty bad and contributing to a lot of the mental health struggles kids are facing today. But keep reading! I will talk about an easy way to make the problem a little better, and it doesn't involve throwing the phone away!

In the 1950s and 1960s, cigarette smoking was huge. Lots and lots of people did it, including kids. At the time, there was not a lot of information out there about smoking, so everyone just assumed it was OK. As time went on, it was discovered that smoking is directly related to many diseases and people should do everything they can to quit smoking. When you ask people who smoked why they did it, their answer many times is, "But we didn't know how bad it was for us."

Unfortunately, I believe we are going to say those same words someday about phones: "We didn't know they were bad." Studies have shown that phones are not only bad for our eyes, sleep, necks, brains, and fingers but bad for our mental health. I have read countless studies on why they are bad, but I don't need to throw a bunch of negative studies at you. I know you have probably heard or read them too. However, as a parent, I can tell you that I one hundred percent see it in my kids when they are on their phones too long. If I am gone for an entire day, I am able to tell you if they spent the whole day in phoneland or a day doing other things. If they were in phoneland they are agitated, quiet, negative, and irritable. As an adult, I even feel these same feelings when I'm on my phone for too long. I describe it as just a "yucky" feeling. But I can adjust since I am able to understand what the phone is doing to me. As a teen, most of you are not quite in tune to this yet, but trust me, it is there.

Did you know that most executives at Facebook, Snapchat, and other social media sites will not allow their kids to be on social media? Even worse, many executives at Apple will not let their kids have phones! What does that say?

One other topic I must address when it comes to phones is sleep. Bottom line, kids do not get enough sleep, and I think it is directly related to phone use for three reasons. One is because you are simply on them too late into the night, and the necessary hours are just not there. Two is because the blue light coming from your phone keeps your brain running even though you have turned it off. So, even though you may fall asleep at whatever time you turn your phone off, you are not getting restful, appropriate sleep. And three is because of the distractions that keep you awake. These are thoughts about a video or show you may have watched, songs running through your head, concerns about a conversation you had with someone, or feelings about a post you may have seen that upset you. It's very hard to turn off those feelings!

So, what's the big deal? I won't get into all of the science, but the bottom line is that lack of sleep is directly related to depression, anxiety, and other conditions. Also, any psychiatrist will tell you that sleep affects the way you handle fear, worry, and stress.

With all of that said above, I am going to give you one suggestion on how to address this issue. I beg you to just give it a try.

"REALITY FOR A DAY" CHALLENGE

First and foremost, you have to want to do this.

Don't do this for anyone but yourself. No one may even know that you are doing this, but I can bet your parents will love it if they find out!

- *Pick a day for the challenge. My kids did it on Sunday because it seems there is not a lot happening on Sunday.*

- *Pick a time to completely turn your phone off. Put it away completely. Don't tell me, "But I need to text my friends for a school project." I'm not buying it.*

- *Message your friends in advance and let them know you are unavailable for the day, just so they know you aren't ghosting them.*

- *Live in reality for the day!*

As much as I hate to have to do this, I think it is necessary. Here are some suggestions of things to do while your phone is off:

- *Make a plan with a friend before the challenge. Face-to-face interaction is so good and is unfortunately dwindling. Talk, laugh, release happy hormones, do dumb things, and be a young person! You will have so much time to stare at screens as you get older.*

- *Did you ever build a leprechaun trap when you were young? Build a trap for your phone. For example, if you try to grab it, you will get mustard dropped on you.*

- *Just think. It's hard to believe, but thinking is good for you and it's a lost art amongst teens these days. It's OK for your mind to be "empty" once in a while!*

- *Dig through cupboards and drawers in your room. You'll find things you have totally forgotten about!*

- *Do some self-care, like using a face or hair mask, drinking a smoothie, taking a long bath, exercising, etc.*

- *Try stargazing. Did you know that this is the one activity that is known to give calming benefits the fastest? Who knew?*

- *Do something you used to do when you were little. Did you like to play piano, shoot hoops, build Legos, or draw? Full disclosure: I secretly played with my Barbies until I was in sixth grade. Don't judge.*

There are some starters for you, but I'm going to make it a little less intimidating. Putting your phone away for a day to help your anxiety probably gives you more anxiety! I get it! So if you don't want to do a whole day, start with baby steps and work up to a day! You can even just try doing it for five minutes at a time.

The one assignment I will ask you to do though, after you complete this challenge, is to check in with yourself and tune in to how you feel. Do you feel less anxious, more relaxed, happier, or alive? Remember, this challenge is not for anyone but you. You don't need to get points at school for it, you don't need to make your parents proud, and you don't need to email me and tell me you did it. You are doing it because you decided to make a change, and you care about yourself enough to do the work. I'm wildly impressed with you already if you have gotten this far in this book.

I want to conclude this section with a personal story about my son. A few weeks ago, he decided that he was eating too much sugar and he wanted to quit. That night, he decided "no more" and went cold turkey. It may sound dramatic when I say this, but it was actually quite scary.

He was agitated, sweaty, and twitchy, and he couldn't sit still. We sort of laughed about it, but he was addicted and was going through sugar withdrawal. As I said before, most of us are addicted to our phones, and while it's not a physical addiction, it definitely will cause some reactions and feelings when you try to give it up. My son got through that night, the next few days, and now feels so much better. He could have grabbed some sugar to make himself stop feeling crappy, but he had to go through the bad to get to the good.

That's something to remember when you try the phone challenge!

CONCLUSION

—

A s I said in the beginning, you may be on a hamster wheel right now, so don't let this book overwhelm you. Maybe just start with one of the breathing exercises. Do it once a day, and get your body ready to do some more work another day.

You now have tools! You have something that you can control. Sometimes, just having possession of something makes you feel like you don't need or want it. For example, imagine if you were outside, and you had a bottle of water with you. If you didn't have it, you might feel really thirsty, but since you do have it, you don't feel thirsty. Or think about if you were at a store, and you had some money in your pocket. Because you have that money, you might feel like you don't want to buy something, but I bet if you didn't have the money, you would really want something badly. Maybe having these tools in your "back pocket" will trick your mind in that way.

Recently, I was having a really "down" day. I couldn't pinpoint why, but I just felt sad. I decided to try to fix it and set out on a walk with my dog. The sun was shining, I had eaten a smoothie for breakfast, and I got a good night's sleep the night before, so the happy hormones should have been flowing, right? They weren't. I tried playing the gratitude game. It didn't work; I still had this unexplainable feeling of sadness. An older couple walked past me, and I gave them a "Good Morning!" The old man smiled a huge smile, and something just clicked in me. Seriously, I instantly felt better and right there decided that I was going to do something for someone else that day; maybe send a struggling friend a message.

If that interaction had not happened and I went home still feeling down, it would have been OK too, but my point here is to keep trying. Keep reaching into that back pocket because you just might find something that will click. However, it may not click, and that is when I think it is important to just embrace your feelings. Why are we concerned if we are not happy all the time? It seems we have gotten to a point where it feels only right to be happy, and if you are not, then something must be wrong. It's not true. Remember in preschool when you were asked,

"How do you feel today? Do you feel sad, angry, happy, or scared?" That's life. Feelings go up, down, and sideways. And that is OK!

There are two things that I continuously see in mentally healthy kids. One is that they have many different interests. The interests don't have to be playing the violin, speaking Spanish, and reciting Shakespeare. They can be loving *Game of Thrones*, liking to fish, and being obsessed with Chick-fil-A. They can be enjoying video games, being interested in cars, and loving your pet. They can be playing basketball, being into a sports team, and hanging with friends. They can be learning how to apply makeup, enjoying interior designing, and exercising.

See the pattern? They can be anything, just something to get you excited, get you going, and get you to enjoy life. Now, you may be thinking, "I have no interests."

Find one.
Search the internet.
Try and try again.
Be curious.

The other thing I see in mentally healthy kids is they have other people to count on. This may be family members, friends, coworkers, neighbors, and teachers. You may think you don't have these people in your life, but you are wrong. They are out there. You just need to put in the work to get to know these people. How about that aunt who lives down the street? Get to know her. What about your favorite teacher at school? Go visit him at your lunch hour or study hall or whenever your school allows this. I promise they will love it; that is exactly why they went into teaching, to be with kids. Reconnect with someone from grade school.

Relationships take work, but they are so greatly important to healthy lives.

Mental health struggles stink, but you are not alone. I bet most of your friends struggle with something or will at some point. You have challenges ahead, but when you conquer some of these issues–WOW–will it feel good! Going through hard times makes a person unique, strong, and confident, and you will get there! My son is at a point where he can confidently say, "I have anxiety, but I know how to handle it." However, it took time.

You did it; you got through the book. Even though I may not know you, I am really proud of you. But more importantly, you should be really proud of yourself.

PROGRESS PAGE

———

Do you know that it takes an average of 66 days to form a new habit? As I've said so many times in this book, you need to do the work. Here is your progress page to work on for the next few weeks. I am not saying it is a cure all, just something to SEE as you work towards helping yourself! Some items you may do more than 2 times, some you may not do at all, up to you!

☐ ☐ gave a hug

☐ ☐ breathing exercise

☐ ☐ turned off phone

☐ ☐ reached a goal

☐ ☐ gave a compliment

☐ ☐ socialized

☐ ☐ laughed

☐ ☐ played with animal

☐ ☐ ate dark chocolate

☐ ☐ spent time in nature

☐ ☐ stargazed

☐ ☐ cold shower
☐ ☐ exercised
☐ ☐ danced
☐ ☐ self care
☐ ☐ made a plan with friend
☐ ☐ sat in sunlight
☐ ☐ got a massage
☐ ☐ completed a task
☐ ☐ played with a baby
☐ ☐ listened to music
☐ ☐ volunteered
☐ ☐ reached out to a friend
☐ ☐ smelled something good
☐ ☐ cried
☐ ☐ stretched
☐ ☐ ate food
☐ ☐ meditated
☐ ☐ reached out to a friend who could use a pick me up
☐ ☐ wrote 3 things down that you are grateful for
☐ ☐ turned 3 negative things into positives
☐ ☐ celebrated a small win for yourself
☐ ☐ did something creative you used to do as a child

QUOTES

———

Q uotes have always resonated with me, and I have collected many over the years that I think are quite good and pretty relevant for teens. My favorite quote of all time and one I truly live my life by is, "You wouldn't worry so much about what others think of you if you realized how seldom they do." by Eleanor Roosevelt.

This one stuck with me, which is why I am sharing my favorites here. Hopefully, one will speak to you in a good way. If so, put it on your mirror in your bathroom, in your car, or even write it on your hand! There are quite a lot of quotes here, so my advice would be to take them in chunks. They may all start to blend together if you read too many at once.

"IF YOU
WANT TO FIND
HAPPINESS,
FIND
GRATITUDE."

"You are exactly where you
are supposed to be."

....

"An ugly personality
destroys a pretty face."

....

"Friendships cause
heartbreaks too."

....

"Peace is not the absence
of conflict but the ability
to cope with it."

....

"If you fell down yesterday,
stand up today."

....

"Be the person you
needed as a child."

....

"Complaining is
not a conversation."

....

"Sometimes, when things
fall apart, they may
actually be falling
into place."

....

"Stop looking for
happiness in the same
place that you lost it."

....

"Happiness comes in
waves; it'll find you again."

....

"I know for sure that what
we dwell on, we become."
(Oprah)

....

"Be gentle with yourself;
you're doing the best
you can."

....

"When you stop
and look around, this life is
pretty amazing."

....

"A negative mind
will never give you
a positive life."

....

"Someday, everything will
make perfect sense."

....

"The realest people don't
have a lot of friends."

....

"Your life is as good as
your mindset."

....

"Keep your face
to the sunshine."
(Walt Whitman)

....

"We worry about
tomorrow like it's
promised."

....

"Forget the mistake.
Remember the lesson."

....

"Stop comparing your
behind-the-scenes
to someone's
highlight reel."

....

"LET GO OF
THE ILLUSION THAT
IT COULD HAVE BEEN
ANY DIFFERENT."

"ASSUME THE PERSON
YOU ARE LISTENING TO
MIGHT KNOW SOMETHING
YOU DON'T."

"If you don't like it, stop putting up with it."

"Do what makes your soul happy."

"When you love what you have, you have everything that you need."

"Creativity is intelligence having fun."
(Albert Einstein)

"People will feel the way they feel."
(LL Cool J)

"Sometimes, happy memories hurt the most."

"Trust the timing of your life."

"The smarter you get, the less you speak."

"People who need the most love will ask for it in the most unloving ways."

"The things you take for granted, someone else is praying for."

"It's cool to be kind."

....

"Have more
than you show,
and speak less
than you know."

....

"Nice words
have the power
to change
someone's life
eternally."

....

"If you are
the smartest person
in the room,
you are in
the wrong room."

....

"Your life isn't yours
if you constantly care what
others think."

....

"The best thing about
telling the truth is that you
don't have to remember
what you said."

....

"People will love you.
People will hate you.
And none of it
will have anything
to do with you."

....

"There are people
who would love to have
your bad days."

....

"DON'T LIVE
THE SAME YEAR
SEVENTY-FIVE TIMES
AND CALL IT
A LIFE."

"THE MORE YOU GROW
INTO A HELPFUL PERSON,
THE HAPPIER YOU'LL FIND
THE WORLD IS."

"Everything
is figureoutable."

....

"Cupcakes are
muffins that believed
in miracles."

....

"If you want a different
result, choose a different
behavior."

....

"We generate the results
in life that we think
we deserve."

....

"There is only one of you
on this entire planet."

....

"Frankly, there isn't
anyone you couldn't learn
to love once you've heard
their story."
(Fred Rogers)

....

"To the world,
you may be one person,
but to one person,
you may be the world."
(Dr. Seuss)

....

"Grief is just love with
no place to go."

....

"We get to choose
who we let into our weird
little worlds."

....

"When you allow
a person's words to hurt
you, you are giving away
your power."

....

"If you don't like
something, change it.
If you can't change it,
change your attitude."

....

"We are what we
repeatedly do."

....

"Grow where you are
planted."

....

"No beauty shines brighter
than a good heart."

....

"May your life be as
awesome as people pretend
to be on Instagram."

....

"Life is rough, so you
gotta be tough."
(Johnny Cash)

....

"We were born to be real,
not perfect."

....

"If you love life, life will
love you back."

....

"The person who tries
to keep everyone happy
often ends up feeling
the loneliest."

....

"THE SECRET OF
YOUR FUTURE IS HIDDEN
IN YOUR DAILY
ROUTINE."

"A LOT OF PROBLEMS
DISAPPEAR IF WE TALK
TO EACH OTHER
INSTEAD OF ABOUT
EACH OTHER."

*"Being alone has
a power that very few
people can handle."*

....

*"What screws us up
most in life is the picture
in our head of how it's
supposed to be."*

....

*"It's better to be the one
that smiled than the one
who didn't smile back."*

....

*"Good things happen.
Love is real.
We will be OK."*

....

*"No one can wear a mask
for very long."*

....

*"Never stop being
a good person because
of bad people."*

....

*"No rich parents,
handouts, or favors.
Straight hustle every day."*

....

*"If I cannot do great
things, I can do small
things in a great way."*
(Martin Luther King Jr.)

....

*"Never judge someone by
the opinion of others."*

....

*"A few nice words can
help a person a lot more
than you think."*

....

*"Life is short. Leave no
lovely word unsaid."*

....

"We rise by lifting others."

....

*"Nothing changes if
nothing changes."*

....

*"Always be a little kinder
than you need to be."*

....

*"Motivation is found when
purpose is discovered."*

....

*"Sometimes peace is better
than being right."*

....

*"If you know
you can do better,
then do better."*

....

"Prove them wrong."

....

*"Be a voice,
not an echo."*

....

*"Enjoy where you
are right now."*

....

*"Having a soft heart
in a cruel world is courage,
not weakness."*

....

"DO MORE THINGS
THAT MAKE YOU
FORGET TO CHECK
YOUR PHONE."

"STOP THINKING
ABOUT WHAT
THEY'RE THINKING
ABOUT YOU."

"A wise person knows there is something to be learned from everyone."

....

"Never get so busy making a living that you forget to make a life."

....

"Sometimes it's OK if the only thing you did today was breathe."

....

"If you aren't grateful for what you have, what makes you think you will be happy with more?"

....

"Judge me when you are perfect."

....

"Cry a river, build a bridge, and get over it."

....

"Be brave. People are rooting for you."

....

"You have to be odd to be number one."
(Dr. Seuss)

....

"Be patient with yourself. Nothing in nature blooms year-round."

....

"There is always, always, always something to be thankful for."

....

"You have one life.
Make it good."

....

"Be kind, for everyone
you meet is fighting
a hard battle."

....

"If you judge
someone, you have no time
to love them."

....

"You are not required to
set yourself on fire to keep
other people warm."

....

"Be the light."

....

"What you see is
what you look for."

....

"I'd rather be hated for
who I am than loved for
who I am not."
(Kurt Cobain)

....

"It's only embarrassing
if you're embarrassed."

....

"It's not about
what you know; it's about
what you do."

....

"You dislike in others what
you see in yourself."

....

"WE ARE ALL A LITTLE BROKEN.
BUT THE LAST TIME
I CHECKED, BROKEN CRAYONS
STILL COLOR THE SAME."

"NO MATTER HOW LONG
YOU HAVE TRAVELED
IN THE WRONG DIRECTION,
YOU CAN ALWAYS
TURN AROUND."

"See good in all things."

*"You teach people
how to treat you."*

*"Stay close to people who
feel like sunshine."*

"Treat yourself gently."

*"No one ever made a
difference by being like
everyone else."*
(P.T. Barnum)

"Be quiet but not blind."

*"What is right is
not always popular,
and what is popular is not
always right."*
(Albert Einstein)

*"People inspire you
or drain you;
pick them wisely."*

*"When you choose
the behavior, you choose
the consequences."*

*"Days are long, but the
years are short."*

*"Don't forget
you are human."*

"The greatest thing in the
world is to know how to
belong to oneself."

. . . .

"Great things never came
from comfort zones."

. . . .

"Life is tough,
but so are you."

. . . .

"You don't have to be
perfect to be amazing."

. . . .

"We grow when things
are hard."

. . . .

"To live is the rarest
thing in the world.
Most people just exist."

. . . .

"Love yourself first,
and everything else
will fall in line."
(Lucille Ball)

. . . .

"We will repeat what
we don't repair."

. . . .

"Breathe. This is
just a chapter, not your
whole story."

. . . .

"What makes you
weird is probably your
greatest asset."

. . . .

"DON'T JUDGE
MY CHOICES WITHOUT
UNDERSTANDING
MY REASONS."

"YOU CAN'T STOP
THE WAVES, BUT YOU CAN
LEARN TO SURF."

"There is beauty
in simplicity."

....

"Today is another
chance to do better."

....

"Confidence is silent.
Insecurities are loud."

....

"Life is short. Smile while
you still have teeth."

....

"You are enough."

....

"Most of the stuff we worry
about never happens."

....

"Own your journey."

....

"Small, healthy choices
make a big difference in
the long run."

....

"Actions speak louder
than 'like' buttons."

....

"Being happy never
goes out of style."

....

"What's coming
will come, and we'll meet
it when it does."
(Hagrid)

....

*"Different doesn't
mean wrong."*

....

*"Everybody has
a chapter they don't
read out loud."*

....

*"You were given
this life because
you are strong enough
to live it."*

....

*"A little consideration,
a little thought for others,
makes all the difference."*
(Winnie-the-Pooh)

....

*"If it feels wrong,
then it probably is."*

....

*"Create a life that
feels good on the inside,
not one that just looks
good on the outside."*

....